WORDS ARE
CHOOSE THEM WISELY

KIND
WORDS ARE
LIKE HONEY

SWEET TO THE SOUL AND
HEALTHY FOR THE BODY.

PROVERBS 16:24 (NLT)

ISBN: 978-1-7371659-1-0
FIRST EDITION JUNE 2021
WORDS ARE LIKE HONEY : BEE KIND

WORDSLIKEHONEY.COM

Dedicated with love
to my ever-so-kind Mom,
Mary Louise Ross.
"Love you...no matter what."
Laurie Allen

You cannot do kindness too soon, for you never know how soon it will be too late.

- RALPH WALDO EMERSON

Be kind whenever possible. It is always possible.

- THE 14TH DALAI LAMA

A part of kindness
consists in loving
people more than
they deserve.

- JOSEPH JOUBERT

Compassion
isn't about
solutions. It's
about giving all
the love that
you've got.

- CHERYL STRAYED

Carry out a random act of kindness, with no expectation of reward, safe in the knowledge that one day someone might do the same for you.

-PRINCESS DIANA

Go and love someone exactly as they are. And then watch how quickly they transform into the greatest, truest version of themselves. When one feels seen and appreciated in their own essence, one is instantly empowered.

- WES ANGELOZZI

A kind gesture
can reach a
wound that only
compassion
can heal.

- STEVE MARABOLI

Kindness can become its own motive. We are made kind by being kind.

- ERIC HOFFER

Human kindness has never weakened the stamina or softened the fiber of a free people. A nation does not have to be cruel to be tough.

- FRANKLIN D. ROOSEVELT

Practice random kindness and senseless acts of beauty.

- ANNE HERBERT

What we all have in common is an appreciation of kindness and compassion; all the religions have this. Love. We all lean towards love.

- RICHARD GERE

You've got to try a little kindness. Yes, show a little kindness.

- GLEN CAMPBELL

Spread love everywhere you go. Let no one ever come to you without leaving happier.

- MOTHER TERESA

Pretty is,
as pretty does.

- ALICE ISABELLE ROSS

As much as
we need a
prosperous
economy, we
also need a
prosperity of
kindness and
decency.

- CAROLINE KENNEDY

Unless someone
like you cares a
whole awful lot,
nothing is going to
get better. It's not.

- DR. SEUSS

Simple kindness may be the most vital key to the riddle of how human beings can live with each other in peace, and care properly for this planet we all share.

- BOB LOZOFF

Constant kindness can accomplish much. As the sun makes ice melt, kindness causes misunderstanding, mistrust, and hostility to evaporate.

- ALBERT SCHWEITZER

No act of
kindness, no
matter how
small, is ever
wasted.

- AESOP

Kindness is the light that dissolves all walls between souls, families, and nations.

- PARAMAHANSA YOGANANDA

Remember there's
no such thing as
a small act of
kindness. Every
act creates a
ripple with no
logical end.

- SCOTT ADAMS

Kind words can
be short and
easy to speak
but their echoes
are truly endless.

- MOTHER TERESA

A smile remains the most inexpensive gift I can bestow on anyone and yet its powers can vanquish kingdoms.

- OG MANDINO

When words
are both true
and kind,
they can change
the world.

- BUDDHA

You can
accomplish by
kindness what
you cannot
by force.

- PUBLILIUS
SYRUS

No one has ever
become poor
by giving.

- ANNE FRANK

To practice five things under all circumstances constitutes perfect virtue; these five are gravity, generosity of soul, sincerity, earnestness, and kindness.

- CONFUCIUS

One thing I do know
for a fact is that the
nicer we are to our
fellow human
beings, the nicer the
universe is to us.

- JOE ROGAN

But love your enemies, do good to them, and lend to them without expecting to get anything back.

- LUKE 6:35 NIV

If you want to
lift yourself up, lift
someone else up.

- BOOKER T. WASHINGTON

Kindness is always in style.

- LAURIE ALLEN

Therefore encourage one another and build each other up, just as you are doing.

- 1 THESSALONIANS 5:11 ESV

Everyone is
fighting a battle
you know
nothing about.
Be kind.

- PLATO

A great man
shows his
greatness in the
way he treats
little men.

- THOMAS CARLYLE

Do your little
bit of good
where you are;
it's those little
bits of good put
together that
overwhelm
the world.

- DESMOND TUTU

Extend yourself in
kindness to other
human beings
whenever you can.

- OPRAH WINFREY

Anyone who knows how to show and accept kindness will be a better friend than any possession.

- SOPHOCLES

I feel the
capacity to care
is the thing that
gives life its
deepest
significance.

- PABLO CASALS

Love and
kindness are
never wasted.
They always
make a
difference.
They bless the
one who
receives them,
and they bless
you, the giver.

- BARBARA DE ANGELIS

When you are kind
to others, it not
only changes you,
it changes
the world.

- HAROLD KUSHNER

Love is patient,
love is kind. It
does not envy, it
does not boast,
it is not proud.

- 1 CORINTHIANS 13:4 NIV

Never be so
busy as to not
think of others.

- MOTHER TERESA

Sometimes it only takes one act of kindness and caring to change a person's life.

- JACKIE CHAN

We can't help everyone, but everyone can help someone.

- RONALD REAGAN

Kind heart, fierce mind, brave spirit.

- ANONYMOUS

A single act of
kindness throws
out roots in all
directions, and
the roots spring
up and make
new trees.

- AMELIA EARHEART

Unexpected
kindness is the
most powerful,
least costly, and
most underrated
agent of human
change.

- BOB KERREY

Kindness begins with the understanding that we all struggle.

- CHARLES GLASSMAN

Kindness is a passport that opens doors and fashions friends. It softens hearts and molds relationships that can last lifetimes.

- JOSEPH B. WIRTHLIN

I just asked,
Is he nice?
Because if he
wasn't kind,
I didn't really
see there was
any point.

- MEGHAN MARKLE
*IN REGARDS TO
PRINCE HARRY*

And as I've gotten older, I've had more of a tendenacy to look for people who live by kindness, tolerance, compassion, a gentler way of looking at things.

- MARTIN SCORSESE

Without tenderness, a man is uninteresting.

- MARLENE DIETRICH

Ask yourself:
Have you been
kind today?
Make kindness
your daily modus
operandi and
change your
world.

- ANNIE LENNOX

But the fruit of the spirit is love, joy, peace, patience, kindness, goodness, faithfulness, gentleness, self-control; against such things is no law.

- GALATIANS 5:22-23 NIV

Kindness is more important than wisdom, and the recognition of this is the beginning of wisdom.

- THEODORE ISSAC RUBIN

Before speaking,
ask yourself:
Is it kind?
Is it true?
Is it necessary?

- MARCY THIMSEN

Happiness is the
new rich. Inner
peace is the new
success. Health
is the new
wealth. Kindness
is the new cool.

- SYED BALKHI

For where there
is kindness there
is goodness, and
where there is
goodness there
is magic.

- CINDERELLA, *DISNEY*

In a world
where you can
be anything,
be kind.

- CAROLINE FLACK

Made in the USA
Middletown, DE
17 June 2021